SMART, Carolyn

Carolyn Smart
BMQO

The Way To Come Home

The Way To Come Home

Carolyn Smart ∽

Brick Books

CANADIAN CATALOGUING IN PUBLICATION DATA

Smart, Carolyn.
  The way to come home

Poems.
ISBN 0-919626-56-4

I. Title.

PS8587.M37W3 1992   C811'.54   C92-093602-4
PR9199.3.S53W3 1992

28/3/94

The support of The Canada Council and the Ontario Arts Council
is gratefully acknowledged.

Cover is after a photograph taken by Kenneth de Kok.

Typeset in Ehrhardt, printed and bound by The Porcupine's Quill.
The stock is acid-free Zephyr Antique laid.

Brick Books
Box 38, Station B
London, Ontario
N6A 4V3

Contents

for Kenneth ∾

The moon and the sun are travellers through eternity. Even the years wander on. Whether drifting through life on a boat or climbing towards old age leading a horse, each day is a journey, and the journey itself is home.

Basho
Oku no hosamichi

Cape of Storms ∾

Yesterday, Today and Tomorrow

Upon one bush, three colours:
powder white, lilac, soft blue, a star
exploding with fragrance

I have opened a door into a new life,
what were the countries I left behind,
a life I thought I was familiar with

In the early morning the ibis flies
to roost, its dark call *Hah-de-dah*
dips a long curved beak
into my dream
draws me from sleep

On the roadside in Hillbrow
a small black child is dancing,
'the time of my life' she sings

The suburbs below drowning
in the thick perfume of flowers,
each walled garden and then the veld
burst open

For my mother, who loved Southern Africa,
although she never went there

We drove at night down Alleman's Kraal Road near the hippo pools. There was a man named Johnson who could see like an owl in the dark. He spoke Shangaan and pointed in amongst the trees: zebra running behind us on the road, red dust drifting in the spotlights. All I could think of was you, mother, who loved to watch the zebra herds running in their paddocks at the Metro Zoo.

Later we ate dinner in the boma, impala meat on skewers and the good red wine of the country. A million southern stars, a sky I never expected to see and did not know my way in. I raised a glass to you then and tried to push away that old grief. Earlier I heard a lioness call to the rest of her pride: a short, low cough as she passed us by, her golden eyes.

In the evening, a woman told me that years ago she was lonely for her small son far away. 'My hands missed him' she said. That too a part of my life now. So much to say to you and no way to say it. I looked up at Centaurus and then turned away, searching the darkness between the lights, filled with the roar of cicadas.

Bluegums

Sheets of rain
stripping the tattered bark,
revealing smooth skin,
white as beluga
Makes you want to place
your cheek against it,
waiting out the storm

In the smoky hills
where coffee grows
the air smells of bluegum,
vibrates with shrill cicadas
On the red earth littered
by torn, bright leaves
we find hoofprints small
as kisses, trail of a duiker
browsing in puddled shade

Buffalo

We would drive on the Open Access Road and then turn off
into the bush at dusk, the warmth of the earth radiating upwards
into our eager bodies, the shy movements of creatures emerging in
shadow.

Pressing on deeper we never knew what we would find, but we
wanted to go into it anyway, whatever it might be. One day we
watched a widow bird for hours. Then, suddenly, a different sort of
darkness, moving, closer: scores of buffalo, their gentle faces and
coiffured horns, the complex boss as if from a delicate mold.

I can barely see the juniper now, ten yards from where I sit. But
once in the Eastern Transvaal I closed my eyes in the night and
listened as a buffalo herd passed by. Here in heavy March snowfall
how can I believe any of this?

Mass Communication

From Sabie to Lydenberg we crossed the mountains at Long
Tom Pass, in imagination watching the British haul their cannon
through the scorched grasses of a summer hillside, the Boer army
always ahead or behind, winning and losing, women and children
dying in the camps built by the British. At the top of the pass I
remembered my father's voice during the Falklands War, denying
news reports of the British strafing Argentinian sailors in the
water: 'British men would not act like that.' Reading *The Fate of
the Earth* at the end of his life, he thought of his safety, his survival
and extinction. Some choose to die with the lies inside them.

Outside Lydenberg we listened to South African Broadcasting
Corporation's Women's Hour and I was thinking of Birmingham
Alabama and that blonde woman quoting biblical chapter and
verse on racial segregation, thereby forming my definition of white
trash forever, and to the drone of SABC's English voice describing
how to make Christmas angels out of napkins we stopped for
drinks in Dullstroom. Puddles of heat on the road and I watched
the woman in the next parked car tell her pale children in
Afrikaans, stay in the car or else, or so it sounded to my untrained
ear, and in the store she bought Cokes and the tabloid featuring Dr.
Christian Barnaard's intended marriage to this or last year's model,
and SABC told us the varieties of street food available in Hong
Kong, and the exact cost of pearls there should you need them, and
Women's Hour signed off for now, and the Christmas carols began.

Christmas In The Bosom Of The Family

My own blood relatives now so few
I stroke their living names
like a square of worn velvet
and now I come to this: grandparents,
cousins, uncles, the extended
family of old friends and their enormous
generosity: Christmas in colonial white Africa

Everything in preparation for The Day
and every morning the floor is washed by the man
who knows me as 'the young madam,'
I learn to refer to myself
in just that way

I dress to choose my gifts,
at the Hypermarket, to compare prices
at Pick 'n Pay and Exclusive Books,
look the wrong way into traffic
and breathe the hot dry air of these
northern suburbs. A young man approaches
with hand outstretched for money,
for the cause of the handicapped he says
as opposed to himself. *Thank you Baas*, he says
to the white man standing next to me
with money in his hand.
Baas an Afrikaans word
for which there is no female equivalent

Christmas in South Africa:
the romance of power,
a birthright honoured
at this time of the year

Driving Through The Drakensberg

Out on the stoep at dawn
drinking coffee, waiting for our lift.
The small boys at the door
calling out 'See you at the beach!'
and then the sun rising over eGoli,
City of Gold: the mine dumps
with their particular kind of grass
hardy enough to grow on chemical waste,
the giant shafts rising over the mines,
much else invisible or disguised.
Now as we drive beyond the city
the late December sun arcs upwards
through the cumulonimbus clouds

What one man does to another
should finally come as no surprise
It goes on as it has done forever

These the names of the places:
Boksburg, Heidelberg, Villiers, Frankfort,
near Reitz the train wreck: dust and shock
of machines in pieces all across the veld,
then Bethlehem, Clarens, Bergville, Winterton,
Loskop, Himeville, Underberg, uMzinto
and the edge of the continent, the sea

The small dog barking from an open door,
black men standing on the dry roads
raise their hands to greet us and smile,
raise Coke bottles to their mouths
Willy Nelson's voice on the tape
and a group begins to sing along
beneath the War Memorial:
the Boer War, the Great War, the Second
World War, the Border War:
For Those Who Died In Glory,
Lest We Forget

Posters for Omo and Lux at the trading stores
in Kwazulu: white women with blue eyes
forever holding up a packet,
lips parted slightly as if about to speak
to the guileless, vacant air

Vultures

When we saw the praying hands postcards at the registration desk we realised that our hotel was a Christian retreat. Later the Minister in charge said 'Tell your friends, spread The Word.' The other guests looked as if they'd spent a long time combing their hair and pressing the creases in their safari suits. The teenaged children were quiet and polite.

When we entered for dinner, a foursome with two bottles of wine, we were the objects of intense scrutiny. We weren't bothered by it until we saw the menu: the cooks could have written the book on pork boiling. We ate the corn, the white bread and margarine, the boiled carrots. We drank all of our wine. Later when we heard them laughing at the wave warnings on the weather report we thought they were laughing at us.

On a mountainside somewhere near Himeville with the sun overhead we stopped the car and got out to look at the valley stretching before us. We were no longer laughing about the night before, and at first were aware only of the slow circular drift of shadows on the dusty road. Shading our eyes, looking up, we saw twenty or thirty vultures soaring above us soundlessly, their dark and tattered wings catching thermals and their beaks pointing down into the valley beneath us.

They were extraordinary, beautiful, gathering in the high heat of the day for something totally unknown to us, and we watched until they disappeared from sight. We drove on, exhilarated, all the way to the sea.

Storms

Think of the myriad small saucers
a storm will mold in a summer ocean
Then imagine the ocean after flood:
clear drops on a sallow surface,
the pallor of a dying man
overflowing with a surfeit of cells
gone wrong everywhere
A woman said she watched
the sugarcane melt off the hillsides
in Natal, pouring down the Umkomaas River
and into the sea

Johannesburg, that city afraid of the dark
Storm rises suddenly in an afternoon of heat,
strips an acacia tree in seconds,
fills a garden with hail the size of golfballs,
floods the streets, the walled enclosures
helpless before the violence blows over
There is steam drifting and the memory of gardens
ankle-deep with ice, enough to carve an image,
here and then gone, just gone

The ocean holds us unfailingly,
a memory before we drew breath
Terrible only this growing desire
to drown in it, to be lost in the ocean,
the raging of the storm

Frangipani

The body embalmed
by odours
from this waxen flower

If I were a girl
I would marry you again
with garlands of this
at my breast
in my hair

The heavy petals
bruising
like skin
on the sand

And always
the ocean at night
undulating
like a tree on fire

Outside the Teahouse of the Blue Lagoon

Past the rich, red soil and the mangrove swamps,
the wild pomegranates that grow near the rocks
and the sluggish bodies of holiday makers
comes the small white child running ahead
of his nanny, a toddler's stumble to the sea
like a tiny geriatric deep in coronary throes,
straight into the water, warm as amniotic fluid
or urine, and he settles into it,
he watches the silt rise up between his toes

Nanny won't let him fall,
the soft tones of her voice protect him enough,
just like her laughter. He wakes at night and knows her
sleeping at his side, on a mat on the floor,
and she sings to him: *Tula um-ntwana, tula*
The first words he speaks are Zulu,
a language like heat or the waves

Mother sits under an umbrella,
her nailpolish matches her sunglasses
One day she went from store to store in Sandton City
taking those glasses out of her purse,
holding them up to the light, late for lunch in the end
and the waiter never got her order right:
Sometimes you are forced to repeat it, slowly,
over and over to be sure they understand
Let me tell you about this morning. I said
you must be up by six, wash both motorcars
before you start the indoor work, then check the roof
for hail damage, see that the gutters are clear,

and don't let me catch you talking to Nanny,
she's got her work to do too, and don't think
there's not others, I said, who would be glad of
your room. Do you know, I'm learning Zulu, so
Ubohlonipha, *and that's a mouthful,*
but I do try.

Nanny lets the small one run to the lagoon's edge
She never glances up towards the mother
or the changeless group in deep umbrella shade,
never takes her eyes off baby
Laughing she holds him to her,
golden child against her starched, white breast

Plantation

The leaves of a banana tree:
old paper and harsh words
unforgiven, they clap in the wind
all day

The boss-boy drowned
at Christmas, drunk
it's presumed,
though there is no autopsy
Near the low dam
where he laughed in the water
the fruit hangs deep
in the mottled light

Chickens peck and scratch
at the feet of children
watching from smoky doorways,
their muddied toes
pointing out into the sun,
dust motes and flies aglow

In shame I turn my face away
I have travelled half way round
this world to sit
with the owners and drink
their cool beer by the pool
Our small blonde children splash
in the clear shallows
while change, that old snail,
paints its sticky, silvered
trail in the hidden places,
everywhere

Ostrich

Driving and getting lost in Blanco
we were laughing at the possibility
of a major tourist attraction;
the largest *dagga* farm in Africa,
and what would it be like to live in a place named
George. I'd always be thinking of my first lover
who later changed his name to something more fitting
a Harlequin romance, someone who gets the girl,
someone named Rock or Lance

Driving down into the Karroo,
heat spangling the pebbled desert
Outdtshoorn: centre of the ostrich world
where you can find a bird's foot
lampstand or an ostrich chick
beneath a bell jar, souvenirs
from a preposterous world, relics
of Hendrik Verwoerd or P. W. Botha

Beyond, in the desert, ostriches are lifting
horned feet around the scrub or settling
absurd, shy bodies into nests of dust and heat
We were still laughing, the way you do
in the face of enormous grief
Oliver Tambo said he had never felt young,
go now and bury your head in the sand

Footprints of a single baboon on white sand

1. Passing zebra and equally exotic birds, we drove over landscape that resembled arctic tundra more nearly than the habitat of wild creatures who live at the Cape of Good Hope.

There was no one about, and when we reached the end of the road we walked down through the rocks to an empty beach tasting the salt sea air and feeling our bodies begin that gentle surrender to the edge of the ocean. Settling down to eat, we broke off chunks of brown bread and dipped them in the soup. I held the hair back from my mouth in the wind.

On the Atlantic side of the Cape, the water is ice cold and opalescent. I walked along the beach feeling that blend of boundless strength and unreality that makes me want to live beside water always. My feet on the white sand, the clear Atlantic foam across my toes. Beyond me, the tracks of a baboon leading down to the water's edge. Then returning inland.

2. The baboon who stands in imagination
   at the lip of the continent
   is a kinder vision than the real,
   a lone, grey creature
   with immaculate fur and intelligent eyes
   who pauses, tail lifted, one paw in air,
   and gazes at the distant vanishing point
   before thinking of home and mate,
   a pile of clams and pawpaws before sleep

   The real one has the head of a dog
   and hair of indeterminate colour
   He feeds on garbage, watching
   everything with crazy eyes
   as if expecting the hand
   of the torturer

   He steals the trash from bins
   and hurls it at passing cars,
   hissing and showing off his teeth
   Arms that could hug you to death,
   hands that could rip you to pieces

   You think of this while your son
   cuddles his soft white monkey toy,
   its eyes unfocussed and ice blue,
   like a dream of the faraway nearby

Cotton / Personal Space

If we had choices the impure could be pure
We wouldn't know that Winston Mankunku's band
works for 50 rand a night at the Club Montreal
somewhere out in Mannenberg, blowing that sax
into weary darkness and the glow of whisky
and the sweat on highball glasses,
intoxication and keen joy. Later we take
deep breaths in the troubled air outside
and lose the rhythm again, driving back
in the night to another part of Cape Town,
each to our separate rooms, in silence

In the windy weather my clothes smell
of sunlight. I am wrapped in sea air
and the constancy of two oceans shaping
the Point: the Cape of Good Hope,
the Cape of Storms: I am wrapped in the weather
and the easeful music, I dress for
the honesty of jazz

In the market of Johannesburg
a slight, clean man slides in front of me
for a view of another band,
to honour township music and much else lost
He stands so close
his shoulder brushes my breast
each time he turns, the softness of cotton
worn thin at the wrists and neck,
the smell of dreaming, of the peace that comes
when a stone eyelid stirs

Poem for a Solitary Baboon

Even when you're alone you carry the presence of others about
you. How I envy you this. I walk onto the beach feeling human
eyes on me. Even with my children I walk alone, my gender lure
enough for violence. But you with your matted fur and enigmatic
sex, you swing to the hood of a car and snatch the proffered fruit.
In the silence surrounding your gluttony, hidden companions are
watching. Their nearness hangs about your shoulders and high
grey haunches as you stalk across the tarmac, curved tail a pennant
in the coastal wind. I cross the littered beach pushing a baby
carriage, fear nipping at my heels. How fast could I run in my lazy
sandals, baby in my arms and a small boy gripped by the wrist?
Lager bottles and the torn wrappings of quick sad meals, cigarette
butts and tins. Tired men with elbows on knees. Vacant eyes. I
stumble and turn for home high on the hill. How I covet your ugly
malice, your body, that naked asylum.

Reaching for the Stars

Some hands more readily form fists
than link ten fingers at the thumbs
in shadowplay, the movement suggesting birds
in flight, something to amuse a child
or even yourself at times

Hendrik Verwoerd was a clever man
who understood the psychology of crowds
'The architect of apartheid'
And when I hear that, I think of
Frank Lloyd Wright in his dark cape
and broad-brimmed hat, his pale tapered
fingers and wild imagination,
the night his cook went mad
and stabbed each guest leaving
that beautiful doomed house, Taliesin.
Verwoerd in his heart divided a society
by the will of God, by pigmentation,
then said that total separation
was an ideal, it was only reaching for the stars

When you hear that old story of a torch
in the dark continent, think about women's hands
swaying over their heads in the smoky gloom
as they listen to Mankunku playing 'Crossroads, Crossroads,'
then remember the fists that claim *Amandla!* there

Hands are more specific to action
than words can be: Verwoerd rising
to speak to those under his sway,
then the surprise of a dagger gripped
in a fist, the arm held high in the air
the thrust at the architect's heart

Statistics from the Annual Report of the Race Classification Board, March 1991

14 Whites applied to be Cape Coloureds (two succeeded)

573 Cape Coloured to be Whites (54 succeeded)

15 Cape Coloureds to be Chinese (nil)

two Whites to be Chinese (nil)

four Whites to be Malay (nil)

10 Malay to be White (one)

three Whites to be Indian (nil)

one Malay to be Chinese (nil)

59 Indians to be Cape Coloured (nil)

17 Indians to be Malay (nil)

33 Malay to be Indian (nil)

four Other Asian to be Cape Coloured (nil)

369 Blacks to be Cape Coloured (42)

two Cape Coloureds to be Black (one)

nine Blacks to be Other Asian (one)

four Blacks to be Indian (nil)

one Black to be Griqua (nil)

13 Cape Coloureds to be Malay (nil)

one Chinese to be Cape Coloured (nil)

10 Indians to be White (three)

23 Malay to be Cape Coloured (23)

five Cape Coloureds to be Griqua (nil)

one Cape Coloured to be Other Asian (one)

Diamonds

Flying into Kimberly, early morning,
the whole town the colour of heat,
of a camel's muzzle as it stands
at the edge of the desert
Thin green leaves of pepper trees
offer as little shade as a twig
Underground the light from diamonds
can blind you with desire

And in a diamond, pastel colours
as if from the bottom of a pool:
bend to it, drink from your own reflection

If you find shade,
lie down in it and take comfort
When you turn your eyes to the sky
all colours seem one
and you are beguiled

At night the boys in the Brothers' College
lie in sheets soaked in cool water
and dream of home
Near the Big Hole the men who labour
for the flash of diamonds
wait for the shift change,
the bite of hot dawn air
and the familiar taste of mealiepap,
to suffer and abide, how long?

mama, mama i am afraid
i fear the elephant outside

(Njabulo S. Ndebele, 'A Child's Delirium')

Fear the one who comes into your home
and is not seen as the enemy
Fear those who feign blindness
and those who say they see

It was not the swift turn of the cheetah
on the River Road at dawn
that caused me fear in that country,
not the elephant that charged us
near the Big Dam –
how we ran for the Land Rover,
the sound of trumpeting behind
as we plunged into darkness,
spider webs in our hair
and giant moths beating against
our foreheads, leaving their soft
magic imprint on our skin

It was not the roadblock near KwaKwa
where men with submachine guns
searched our car for arms
and we watched the snipers sitting
in silence on the hillside

It was the night the young men talked of the future
when the Boer would work for them,
how it was one's obligation to hire Blacks
but not to pay them a living wage.
Oh shit, we're not worried about the Blacks,
we're worried about the sliteyes
And the women in the room laughed
and charmed them. Then I knew I was an orphan
and very far from home, lonely
and appallingly afraid
And at another dinner, the man on my left,
asked his answer to 'the coloured problem':
Bomb the townships, kill all the kaffirs, and start again

Burn Down the Fynbos

1. Hout Bay

I saw your photograph in the morning paper,
the face of a man of indeterminate age,
a man who has lived his life in the shelter
of whatever he could carry on his back:
the corrugated iron roof, the powdery timbers,
at night the Port Jackson willow flicking back and forth
over the fingers of the wind, the sweet smoke
curling up into sea air, the white sand beach
in a place so privileged the whites call it
The Republic of Hout Bay
and the ANC moves squatters in
to try and spread the wealth a little,
if by perceived imposition or even shame

But shame is not what I saw in your face, old man,
your mouth wide with shock, the skin
in bubbles on your back and shoulder blade,
a wing torn away before it could unfold,
the settlement burned and the firemen,
in strange Victorian pantomime,
the silver tipped helmets of the Empire abroad,
turning on their hoses while you and others
gathered rocks in your fists to hurl,
thinking of all uniforms
as of police in yellow vans
a history of death

2. Hermanus

There's a painting by David Hockney,
one of his swimming pools, and the blue of the water
matches the blue of the sky in Hermanus,
the sugar birds with their elongated beaks
sipping the nectar from the fynbos:
flowers that would decorate a moonscape,
Tony calling to the birds and they responding,
back and forth across the hot clifftop

The house with the Hockney
sits on the cliff edge. As we walked
and smoked our cigarettes we laughed
and chose this house for Thabo Mbeki
when the revolution comes,
nearly tossing a lit match into the scrub
and watching it all burn down.
Let's start again right from the beginning

The fire that swept down the mountain
on the outskirts of Hermanus,
the squatters burned out, the straw shacks,
the wooden huts, the bricks of the three pigs
consumed by flame,
the black scar on the hillside it left behind
would snatch the breath from your lungs

Sometimes I am filled with so much anger
there is no conflagration large enough
for all I want to burn

the women is bathing ∾

if the women is bathing

    if the women is bathing, suppose you coming on, they see you
coming on there and they having a bath in the river and they are
naked. Don't figure that they are going to hide their puss. They're
going to hide their breasts. I ask them, I say, 'But why you hide
the breast? You should hide the other special part.' They said, 'No,
no, no, no. We born with that, so you can see that as you like, but
we didn't born with this.' That's why they hide the breasts.

What Happen, A Folk-History of Costa Rica's Talamanca Coast,
edited by Paula Palmer

Avocado

That night I ate
the finest avocado, smooth
as the folds of skin
on a baby's neck and sweet,
the way Daniel smells of milk and salt
in memory of tidal buoyance;
in the early morning I saw the ocean
gunmetal grey and the dark green leaves
that hide pale parrokeets,
the mirror of a heart's tender fruit,
its technicolour promise
and subtle taste, a mouthful of velvet,
Daniel's warm hands at my neck,
his solemn eyes
and skin the colour of my breasts,
tropical air, I was eating the food of life

the woman, bathing

1. what I wanted

to slip into that ocean in the early morning with the sea clear
and my head filled with clouds, I wanted the water to slip over me
like a tongue, like a kiss that filled in all the painful places, I
wanted to be held by my mother, I wanted to be alone, I wanted
peace and the deepest green I could imagine and the curve of a line
of pelicans flying over in the simple light, I wanted the salt in my
mouth and hair and afterwards to feel it on my skin like that thin
dress I have never found, the echo of waves breaking on the beach,
sand like Canadian winter, my heart in my skin, and the moment
when the grey wave met me and, breathless, I thought of not
coming back

2. what happened

I walked over the red tile floor of the Flamingo Beach Hotel.
The halls were dark and cool and at the end of the row of softly
decorated rooms there was a small white verandah where people
gathered at sunset to drink guanabana daiquiries and gaze absently
at each other, middle-aged, middle-class tourists somewhat
confused as to where they were in the Central American scheme of
things.

I walked down the hot cement steps and out into the blaze of
sunlight. Over my shoulder I carried the beach bag each traveller
had been given ten days previously as we stood in the chaos of
spring break, Pearson Airport, six o'clock Saturday morning. In the
bag I was carrying sunscreen to protect my small pale children, my
point-and-shoot camera so as to record not only the snow white
beach but the houses of the rich Costa Ricans overlooking the
beach and the glowing faces of my children as they scampered in
and out of rock pools and jumped the warm waves of the ocean. At
the bottom of the bag were two room keys, a baby's hat that I
hoped to be able to keep on his head a few seconds at a time, and
my own beach cover-up that perhaps I'd have the inclination to use
if I had the energy for a swim, should I get up from the beach and
walk down to the water a few steps away.

My sunglasses kept slipping down my nose. My whole face felt
coated in some kind of mask and my hair stuck out like straw in the
salty air. The night before I'd woken every hour to hold the baby.
At times it felt as if I hadn't slept at all, yet I knew I'd opened my
eyes every once in a while and been surprised to find myself in
such surroundings, and that meant I'd been somewhere else, in a
dream or subtle reverie.

3. the dream

standing on the side of the road in San Jose she walked
backwards just a few steps to sit on the edge of a low stone wall.
Bougainvillea was growing there in various shades of red and
fuchsia. She looked up to see a long V of Canada geese flying north.
She could see their eyelashes, their glistening liquid eyes.

4. how it was

I walked past all the other guests sitting by the pool, across the sandy road and down onto the beach. In the distance I could see two boys climbing the mangrove trees, and sitting in their shade there was a dark-skinned man holding a very pale, blonde baby. I walked closer to them, the shoulder bag bumping gently against my breasts, and I felt the milk coming down into my nipples make that tiny bluewhite marbling beneath the skin. I knew, even now with my head full of sleep and the wind in my eyes, that I wasn't waiting for anything else, any more. I knew I was living my life, at last.

Fiesta / Tree of White Birds

A fiesta is a carnival
that smells of beer,
beer spilled in dust bowls
and raised to lips parched
from sucking limons
and abuse of poor cattle,
their bovine ears and hangdog eyes
bred for the tropics
and the shade of umbrella trees

The trees we pass
as we drive to the fiesta
are thin and blonde like models
From one hangs the effigy
of a policeman who guards
the ballot box all day
Bad spirits at work here, maleficios,
there are bells and feathers waving,
noiseless clapping in the warm sea air

Nicholas and I take a sky ride in
a red metal box with no restraints
Our mouths bite holes in the air
as we rock ungently, squeezing our sides
I hear his small voice from my armpit:
'please stop, sir, please make it stop,'
as if carnival and rape were one,
as if a maleficio would stop at one's wish,
at the sound of a tender plea – have mercy

We bump along the beach road,
Nicholas with his head on my arm
our faces flushed with wind,
smoke from controlled burning all along the hillsides
The sun low, his head falls in sleep to my knees
and there, look: a tree full of white birds,
too weary now for flight

Walking to the Ocean: Dawn

I am too tired for sentimentality,
and the ocean looks cold, so
I press your cheek to mine, Daniel,
and we walk out along the promenade –
you held high in my arms

It seems natural to be lost in the roll of waves
and the sawing of insects,
all night to lie hearing this,
then stand up and walk to the ocean
while the heat grows around us
like a room filling up with parachutes

Hold my hand now, Daniel,
your plum-size fist
and darkening lashes precise as flames
When the doctor cut me open
and saw you crouching there
my tenderness spilled out
Grey, wet boy they pummelled into life,
what do words like need or sorrow
mean to you, full or less, my care
for you all in this outstretched hand

We walk to the empty beach,
I am thinking cleanly of your birth
How could I have imagined
a love as artless as this

Hunger for the Next Thing

I swam with my children in the ocean
and felt their need like an undertow,
felt my breasts swell
to fill the necessary luminous cones
so many mouths had made
with their calling and their limited
attentions

I lay with my head buried in my arms
and listened while the CNN broadcast
stories of local interest to America
Lastly Daniel Ortega, weeping,
the election lost,
or perhaps the tears were mine, but
the children were greedy for cartoons,
where pale chinless characters
die a thousand deaths an hour

Outside, the buses filled with workers
and the daylight faded. Elsewhere
lights went on all up the hillside
and the alcoholics knew a fresh thirst
Each small star swallowed up the blackness
round about, the children clambered
about my legs and pulled at my clothes,
apparel of the materfamilias:
my loving anger, my ravening heart

The Sound of the Birds ∽

for Bronwen Wallace

Death may indeed be the last great foe of writing, but writing is also the foe of death.

J.M. Coetzee, *Age of Iron*

Whip-poor-will,
voice in the night woods:
by day, when disturbed, they say
you flee like a large brown moth
Each night I listened for your call,
each night and every night
when your call stopped
I held my breath, suspended,
for fear of an end to this,
this intimate acquaintance,
a quickening of breath itself

1. *Owl, Loon and Thunderstorm*

Driving home that day as on all other days,
through country as familiar
as the bones of my face,
reaching often to my cheeks
and drawing my fingers down through
history, trying to wipe away awkwardness
or scars of the past, but that day
near Elginburg and the herd of pale Charolais
I drove into a storm like lilacs in full bloom,
Cimmerian darkness, you, dying,
and I but witness to the end

The faces of stranded drivers that I passed
I didn't understand til later, when the storm
had cleared and I was on dry ground;
I searched the roads for catastrophe
as if these strangers' shattered visages
held something I knew
but had not seen yet,
all summer driving into it,
this future of unbearable sadness,
holding my newborn son in my arms
while I sat by your bed, you and I weeping,
the sound of many birds calling
and the poplar leaves scratching against
the wooden fence: everything I knew useless
against this catastrophe

Rising at night I'd lift Daniel from his crib
and fall into a chair by the window,
place him on my breast,
think of you awake in pain and thirst
I'd grow accustomed to a dialogue with silence,
then wait for the sounds of night

First, the heavy movement
I called 'owl,' unsteady steps, then silence
In the morning I found castings on the warm day ground
below my northern window
Later I'd hear the calls of other nightbirds hunting
They were far shriller than my fears,
I wanted whispers while I sat and listened in the night,
felt my heartbeat, the small insistent lips,
heard his tiny breath, remembered
the sound of air whistling through
the dark hole of your cheek

One night I heard the loons cry
all the way from Knowlton Lake,
a clear cool night without wind:
it made me believe you'd survive this,
this indescribable evil,
squamous cell carcinoma,
the black cancer on your face

2. *Cardinal and Lunar Eclipse*

The red bird
and then silence, while I sat
and watched all you endured:
the raw eyes of those afraid to touch you,
doctors who spoke as if you were not there,
months of radiation, pus that filled your mouth,
treatments that failed again and again,
pain that was never controlled, and then
the other things, the thirst and hunger,
your white eyelet nightgown pulled up
exposing your thighs, injections of laetrile,
that look in your eyes,
a terror I have never seen before,
your individual vision of death

I have cancer of the mouth,
you wrote over and over that first day
in your journal, as if by repeating
you might begin to believe it, conquer it
separate it from your future

That cardinal would catch my eye
as I sat on your couch downstairs,
Daniel sleeping in his swing
and the tick of the wall clock
continuous and taunting, broken by
bird calls, the scratch of their beaks
as they darted here and there for food,
red flash of the northern cardinal, its black
eyes and throat, bright moments
in these dark summer days

Later I'd see that red
as a bloom growing in your pale throat,
the arterial blood, hovering
barely beneath the skin that glowed
as I entered your room, breathless
with eagerness and grief
All things became real in one place,
the earth and beyond centred there

Full lunar eclipse:
I stood in the darkness and watched
the shadow creep across
your glowing features,
while all others round about me
watched the marvel in space
I watched you die,
gripping my baby to my chest
I let you go over and over,
still breathing the possibility of miracle

3. A Dream and a Turkey Vulture

After all the radiation was finished and they offered you the name of a doctor in palliative care, one night you dreamed there were still more treatments and you were standing naked in a circus tent. A crowd was throwing balls at you. In desperation you reached for your gown, unable to put it on. 'It doesn't matter whether you're protected or not, anymore' your doctor said. A circus tent. A hostile crowd. Doctors that do no good at all. You dream and then you wake.

panic, feeling of being written off, these are good doctors, but once their skills can't help, they see nothing, cannot learn from me

Early in July I drove with my son Nicholas out into deeper country. The sun was sharp and the land golden as befits a place where summer falls all in one day. On the road, a dead rabbit, its dark skin marred by trailing pink intestines. A vulture lifted its black feet from the gravel pavement, its naked head swivelling.

4. *Eastern Phoebe*

Small tail-bobber,
when it was not fly-catching
it was (*Phoe-be*) announcing itself
the way I wanted to,
shouting out my self
as if that might halt the dreadful,
unstoppable growth of what
I saw first as a red ball on your cheek,
then as the creature that was
killing you, filling your house
with the smell of cancer

The look in your eyes
is what I lived with,
the eyes of exhaustion
from an argument with death,
eyes after hours of tears,
whole nights of fear and pain
while you lay awake waiting for
the first bird that called forth the light,
the memory of ordinary mornings,
just the sun and coffee
and Jeremy and Chris off into
their days, the house settling down,
the poem coming on

you wrote, four days before your final, slow breath,
and now this absence, this silence

I'd sit on the verandah in the early evening,
remembering, holding Daniel, watching the sky
and the Phoebe dipping for insects along
brief thermals that made us once
believe in angels;
I wanted their firm, warm beating bodies to hold
in my hand and give to you
as a supplicant might offer up
her breath for yours,
to do what was impossible
for us, poor humans, slaves to gravity

Then at night, waking with Daniel's cry
for a moment I thought I'd dreamt all this,
would see you well, untouched,
free, oh Phoebe,
sweet dipping bird
my heart bleeds for my friend

5. Cockatiel

The nervous chatter reduced to a breath
bated, blood coursing round your lucid
brain, sound of the morphine pump
like a frenzied electric insect,
your hand rising slowly to your cheek,
pressing the white bandage
into place, resting briefly
at the dark shadow of blood
on your translucent neck,
your fine fingers never more beautiful
than now, I kiss them, watch their continuous
flicking movement as you hold your straw
in ice water that never slakes the thirst

The calling of the cockatiel downstairs
mixes briefly with Daniel's cry. When I leave you now
I turn briefly at the door,
your lean body on the bed
forever in that room burnt into my sight,
my waking moments and my sleep
all focussed there

A small bell in the cage:
he rings it with his head,
side to side, lifts his yellow eye to me,
shining. He opens his pale beak, and screams
in imitation of those on the wing outdoors

Daniel smiles as I raise my clothes,
let loose my milk,
tears, the garden offering up its gifts,
late summer afternoon,
the dusty smell of poplars before rain

whip–poor–will,
where is your voice now?
Animals are furtive in these briefer days,
high limbs of trees grey, rapt in concentration
for the sap's retreat,
even the stars seem aloof
and you are not here, dear night bird,
you are gone

the stillness is a room I've moved into,
like the clothes I will wear
to ward off colder weather,
a cape of loneliness,
the dark heart of a night without song

Home : A Calendar ⌒

November: Frontenac County

Trees are dark fountains of grief
moaning *summer, summer*
in damp and breathless voices,
at the place where they pull free
from soil, piles of leaves weep
in their repetitious way,
a haven for nothing

Even the porcupine swings
its quills away in scorn
and continues its solitary parade
towards the frost and shelter

A doe with excitable ears
wide open for the hunter's tread
stands in a sodden field,
steam rising from its nostrils
as we pass, marvelling

All the flowers of summer in memory:
we want to fill our cups
with potpourri and sleep
It is November, and we yearn
for flight

December Garden

Sad weeds, snagged in snow,
how I have neglected you!
The bowls of wilted blooms left over
from a funeral. When I walked away
from my mother's body in the predawn light,
I knew afterlife was what I carry with me in memory,
in the way I put my arms around a friend
and feel the warmth of those gone,
their round shoulders, soft breasts

On a winter night I always look to the sky,
this northern hemisphere where now
the sky is often upside down to me,
clear stars and wise blue space beyond
If I could talk to the dead!
Once I heard my voice on radio,
zebras and their sorrowful echoes
soaring out and out
The dead, listening

Tonight I watch late airplanes on cruise
to European destinations, technology
in Christmas wrap slowly flashing by,
reflecting colours in my winter garden
Senses aching for summer,
tattoo of rain on maple leaves,
sudden smile of one who was a stranger
now welcome at the door of my home

Winter Moon: January
(for Daniel)

Midnight, and the view from the upper window glows. It is a
candle held to an egg, it is my son floating within me, my body in a
close warm room looking down on snow that is blue, blue as the
lining of a cloak embroidered with stars. In the shadow of the cedar
boughs small animals forage in silence. There are many things I
cannot see, yet honour, like the unheld hands that reach me from
the inside, limbs and their white lanugo. I hear Nicholas and
Steffen calling from their dreams. The earth is held in blue light
before dawn. I am standing at the window, six months pregnant.
Now it is well past midnight. I am closer to prayer than breathing.

February: Driving in labour
(for Nicholas)

Filled with a terrible energy. I stared out the windows into the earliest of mornings, the stretches of prickly ash and sugar maple, the quiet spaces amidst the trees where timid creatures take shelter. I was fearful that I would not love this baby, this stranger that I opened my body for, months ago, in love. It was as if I had waved aside the history of the world, the history of my parents with their hard faces and self-denial. Now Kenneth and I were driving in the snowy predawn towards the hospital, my belly a stubborn fist, unruly tongue. Suddenly an owl arced towards the windshield, white like a snowy but huge and tufted like a great horned. Its yellow eyes steady. Swift pale bird and the white Ontario winter. My desire for the future soared through that February night.

March thaw, March snow

Earth brown, earth softening,
this warm sudden soil
that lets its thrills out,
emergent early crocuses in my garden,
their white tongues poking
unbidden from the loam:
pale children, tentative and lean,
summer's hope a linen napkin
held to the lips, once, softly

Then snow again, autumn's chill breath,
the mossy tree's promise withdrawn,
willows bending to the pond's cold face
They weep for us, without shame
down the leafless avenue,
where now the silver clump of birch
goes on to wave its stiff dry pennants
at a white and bare reflection

April: preparing the beds

When spring peepers trill from the pond
and the first day comes clear, without chill,
I am outside, uncovering the front beds,
raking out sodden leaves, displaying
the heads of sedum like brussel sprouts,
and the phallic tips of hyacinth: such gifts!
Last year, with Daniel ready to be born,
I scrabbled at the soil as now,
blessing green, growing giddy
with the new April air. That night Daniel turned,
his head beneath my ribs,
one foot in air and one drawn down by gravity,
toenails tearing at the sack of waters, and me
lying later on a hospital bed, crying,
while the woman next door mourned her stillborn:
take it out, take it out,
and Daniel's heart beat strong and eager;
they placed him shining wet against my cheek,
his round eyes and soft white facial hair;
for a week I saw his pale limbs under lights
Outside there was the Murney tower,
Wolfe Island, the ferry's steady pace,
dark blue water, the scudding clouds above,
the garden at home, dark with other promise

May

May is a watercolour, a book of drawings
abandoned in the grass;
a mist of appleblossom and lilac
Marshmarigolds, treasure tossed
at the feet of mossy trees
Trilliums, with their soft bruised charm
and the yellow or blue of childish violets
The tall sugarmaples, their elegant display,
a panoply of green

We lie down in a tango of night and warmth
as if the deep scent of earth
in spring were not miraculous,
as if our monochrome winter
with its constant dirty chill
did not make hunger in our mouths
like an ache, now a vague ghost,
like a mosquito's late-night hum
when your eyes are closed to the dark

Listen now to pond's heartbeat,
the shrill monotony of spring peepers
calling goodnight and goodnight,
over and over, to everything
that is beginning, or is no more

June: the Green and Silence

Today so still I can hear a robin move
among the new-growth maples,
the occasional puff of wind embraced
by high, mottled branches

Last night we woke to hear light rain,
or so we thought: the sky was clear
and by the bright moon we knew it was
caterpillars eating their fill,
the leaf shit falling and falling
on translucent patterned webbing,
all they left of the sugarmaple leaves

Two nights ago I sat and talked
with Nicholas before story and then bed
We found a luna moth at rest
outside the window: what a breath I took
at the sight of it!
Tonight he taps the screen,
we watch it fly

In *A Field Guide to Moths* it says
'Wings: pale green,
transparent spot on each,'
which does not catch the thing at all,
how it defines etherea and grace,
and in the photo they have pinned it
to a pale blue sheet,
wings outstretched, the double spots
like hindsight, second sight some say

July Heat

Very early morning
From Daniel's western window
I watch the hummingbird
in amongst the solemn hollyhocks,
he with his ruby throat against
their mute pastels

A slow breeze stirs the Midnight Lilies,
those spectacular hybrids I gentled into loam
late last year, weeping for my friend,
but now there is no weeping.
The sound of haying drifts
towards me through the spruce and pines
as if our rocky, soil-poor hill
were nuzzled up against the salty ocean foam

In the heat of noon, drowsy snakes lie
fat and dark beneath the granite rocks
that mark the drive, the shriek
of cicadas breaks the midday open
the way lightning cracks a dream
when I've failed to anticipate the storm

The Place We Come to Call Home: August

North of Elginburg,
the heavy Charolais steers
flick their tails in dry hot yards
and my heart turns
The road from the ridge to the highway
is lined with magenta and violet wildflowers,
a carpet on the rocky waste:
Purple Loosestrife, St. John's Wort
In this same dusty spot bouquets of Feverfew
blossomed in June. Now Rod Wallace's dairy herd
moves slowly through the cedar

When was that day I knew I belonged here,
felt that familiar ache I once confused
with adolescent happiness, driving with my mother
years ago. 'Hey Jude' played for me alone
whenever we listened to radio

This land began to sing for me last summer
driving from the ridge where we raise our children
awkwardly in love with the space and violent weather,
marvelling at the political intentions of the neighbours
and the avarice of those who sell their front fields
and insularly complain about immigration

Here I take refuge in tree configurations,
the slow drift of withered leaves to soil,
the flocking of grackles sensing
summer's end, the speech of owls as I sit
with Daniel in a warm blue chair before dawn,
not quite awake, but listening, fully alive

Jetstream: Late September

Half way between McGreer's Groceries
and the post office
I hear the geese
The brain stores everything somewhere,
they used to say,
an imprint
The more you hear something
the deeper the memory,
old memories, layer upon layer
in the grey cells of the cortex,
one over the other
like feathers on the wing
Slip a scalpel into the brain
in the precise place
and maybe reproduce
the sound of two hundred geese
flying over in something resembling a V
I hear them long before I see them
and when I see them, I want to weep:
October and they're gone;
April, and they return,
bringing colours back,
a green so tender, the new leaves
folding over and bending,
the wind picking up and carrying
the leaves, birds, soil smell
I can barely see the geese with the sun
in my eyes. I want to be going somewhere
The southern hemisphere
where water turns clockwise
right down to the sea,
all along the horizon: birds, clouds,
sunset, sunrise, all the same time

October

Those fallen leaves, pale supplicants,
have much to teach us of surrender,
how, wrapped in autumn's incense
they unfurl their flags to the wind

Every year I want to kneel in damp soil
and say farewell to blessed things:
the swift geese as they shout each to each
above the treetops, the white nicotinia
at my door, still releasing its fragrance
against the chill of evening,
the memory of a much-loved hand
the last day I held it

There was early morning light rich as silk,
the flash of late fireflies
amidst the cedar,
cows' tails whisking in the amber fields,
the chiaroscuro of a moth's wing

Goodbye, brief lives,
ablaze with tenderness;
today the glory of the leaves
is enough, for I am learning anew
to release all I cannot hold,
these moments of luminous grace
saying Here and here is beauty,
here grief: this is the way to come home

Notes on the poems

p. 6: Yesterday, Today and Tomorrow: shrub with flowers at first purple then lavender-mauve and then finally white, so that all three colours are finally seen on the bush at the same time.

p. 7: boma: enclosure, often of thorn bush, to protect camp or animals. (Swahili)

p. 8: duiker: a knee-high, grey or reddish antelope widely distributed throughout the montane forest regions of South Africa.

p. 11: Baas: master, boss, employer; title or form of address. (Afrikaans)

p. 17: Tula um-ntwana, tula: Hush, baby, hush. (Zulu)

p. 18: Ubohlonipha: Be respectful. (Zulu)

p. 20: Dagga: Marijuana. (Khoi)

p. 23: when a stone eyelid stirs: Elisabeth Eybers, Afrikaans-speaking South African poet, from her poem 'Pygmalion.'

p. 25: Amandla: power (Zulu) Often shouted at political demonstrations: amandla ngawetu: power is ours.

p. 29: kaffirs: any Black person, now an actionable insult.

p.31: Thabo Mbeki: member of the ANC Executive; one of the most prominent of the ANC younger generation.

p.47, 49 & 50: all passages in italics are drawn from Bronwen Wallace's last journal.

Acknowledgements

Some of these poems first appeared in: *Event, Matrix, Poetry Canada Review, The Canadian Forum, The Malahat Review, The Kingston Whig-Standard, This Magazine,* and *Quarry.* Some were broadcast on CBC Radio's 'Morningside' programme.

I'd very much like to thank the following people who helped me in the reworking of some of these poems: Robin Benger, Kenneth de Kok, Susan Glickman, Merilyn Simonds Mohr, Erin Mouré, and Bronwen Wallace. Finally I want to thank my editors Stan Dragland and Marnie Parsons for their perseverance and hard work during those hilarious evenings at Depot Creek, and for helping me to make this collection as honest as I had hoped it could be.

KENNETH DE KOK

Carolyn Smart was born in England in 1952 and moved to Canada with her parents and sister in 1958. She has since lived in Ottawa, Toronto, and Winnipeg, and moved to the country north of Kingston in 1983. Since 1985 she's lived on a farm between Sydenham and Harrowsmith, Ontario. She and her husband Kenneth are raising three children: Steffen (12), Nicholas (8) and Daniel (3).

Carolyn's previous collections of poetry have been *Swimmers in Oblivion* (York Publishing, 1981), *Power Sources* (Fiddlehead Poetry Books, 1982), and *Stoning the Moon* (Oberon Press, 1986). Her non-fiction essays have appeared in *Fireweed, Quarry*, and *Best Canadian Essays 1989*. She has worked as an editor at Doubleday Canada and Macmillan's, been a member of the Editorial Collective of *Fireweed, A Feminist Quarterly*, edited the Manitoba Budget Address in 1974 and 1975, sold women's clothes in the Eaton's Centre and at Harrods, reviewed poetry for magazines and newspapers across Canada, and worked as a freelance editor. Since 1989 she has taught Creative Writing at Queen's University.